A big thanks to the researchers who helped with this project, and of course to the mammoths who have offered up their bodies to science — S. P.

First published in North America in 2005 by
Two-Can Publishing
11571 K-Tel Drive
Minnetonka, MN 55343
www.two-canpublishing.com

Translated and adapted by Gwenyth Swain
Edited by Jill Anderson
Cover design by Joe Fahey
Illustrated by Charles Dutertre, Xavier Mussat, Julien Norwood, Riad Sattouf, Mathieu Malot

Originally published in France by Tourbillon S.A.R.L. under the title *Les dessous du mammouth.*
Copyright © Tourbillon, 2004.

Library of Congress Cataloging-in-Publication Data

Philippo, Sophie.
[Dessous du mammouth. English]
Meet the woolly mammoth / by Sophie Philippo ; [translated and adapted
by Gwenyth Swain ; illustrated by Charles Dutertre ... et al.].
p. cm.
Summary: "This book explains how scientists study woolly mammoth remains and
what we know about these extinct land mammals"—Provided by publisher.
Includes bibliographical references and index.
ISBN 1-58728-521-5
1. Woolly mammoth—Juvenile literature. I. Swain, Gwenyth, 1961–
II. Dutertre, Charles, ill. III. Title.
QE882.P8P4713 2005
569'.67—dc22
2005007818

1 2 3 4 5 6 10 09 08 07 06 05

Printed in France

Photo and Illustration Credits: p. 9: North Sea, © 2001, F. Latreille/Cerpolex; p. 10, left: Gesner's Horn, K. Gesner, Icones animalium quadrupedum vivparorum et oviparorum..., 1560, © MNHN (Muséum National d'Histoire Naturelle, Paris) Central Library; p. 10, right: Giant, A. Kircher, Mundus Subterraneus..., 3rd edition, 1678, © MNHN-Phanérogamie Library. Negative, P. Lafaite; pp. 10-11: Leibniz Unicorn, Summi polyhistoris G.G. Leibnitii Protogaea, 1749 © MNHN-Central Library; p. 15, Mammuthus Expedition, "The Ice Block Containing Jarkov Is Lifted by Helicopter," © 1999, F. Latreille/Cerpolex; pp. 18-19: M. Adams Skeleton, Recherches sur les ossements fossils de quadrupèdes, 1825, G. Cuvier © MNHN-F. Petter. Negative, P. Lafaite; p. 29, upper left: © Ministry of Culture and Communication, DRAC Rhône-Alpes. Regional Archaeological Service; p. 29, upper right: © Denis Vialou, with the kind permission of the town of Cabrerets; p. 29, lower left: © O. and J. Plassard; p. 29, lower right: © Institute of Archaeology, ASCR (Academy of Sciences of the Czech Republic), Brno.

Meet the
Woolly
Mammoth

by
Sophie
Philippo

MINNETONKA, MINNESOTA

Contents

Introducing...Mammoths!

How can we get to know mammoths? These huge elephant-like beasts died out, or became **extinct,** thousands of years ago, so we can't meet them face-to-face.

When folks can't see an animal alive, they tend to wonder about it. That's certainly been the case with the mammoth. Was the mammoth mean? What did it look like? How much did it weigh? Did it like to eat peanuts? Where did it live? What did it do all day long? And what did it *taste* like?

Mammoths aren't the great-grandparents of Dumbo or Babar. They aren't very, very old elephants with big heads, although they are related to elephants. They lived at the same time as early humans, but not at the same time as the dinosaurs. Dinosaurs had already been extinct for millions of years! The last mammoths lived at the same time as the great Pharaohs of Egypt, but in lands so far away that King Tut never met one.

Mammoths lived in parts of North America and **Eurasia,** including South Dakota, France, and Siberia (see pages 38-39). They were some of the most mammoth—or biggest—animals ever to roam the earth. There were once several kinds, or **species,** of mammoths. The best known of these was covered with a thick, woolly coat that kept it warm and gave it its familiar name: the woolly mammoth.

We still have a lot to learn about these animals. But the more **fossils** we uncover, and the more frozen, fur-covered mammoth bits we dig up in Siberia, and the more closely we study all mammoth remains, the more we get to know this great beast. Someday we may be able to solve the mystery of why the woolly mammoth—actually, *all* mammoth species—disappeared.

For hundreds of years, villagers and just plain folks out for walks have discovered mammoth bones. These bones have been found in fields, near caves, or sticking out of cliff-sides around Eurasia and North America. Because mammoth bones are so large, their discovery often led to lots of head-scratching among the locals.

In Siberia in the 1700s, hunters looking for reindeer would sometimes stumble upon mammoth tusks sticking out of the frozen ground. Some hunters cut the tusks off and sold them in the nearest village. People began to buy and sell the ivory from these tusks (used for billiard balls, piano keys, statues, and jewelry), and that business continues to this day.

What's the best tool for finding mammoth remains? Phil Anderson, a land developer in Hot Springs, South Dakota, might answer, "A bulldozer." In 1974, one of his bulldozer operators accidentally dug up a **sinkhole,** or depression in the ground, where mammoths once came to bathe and drink. Thousands of years ago, some of the animals became trapped, and their bodies became fossilized. These animals were North American cousins of the woolly mammoth.

What's Left of Mammoths

Bits and pieces of mammoths have been found—and continue to be found—stuck in frozen ground, covered in water in a sinkhole or in the sea, jutting out of a cliff, or lying in the open air of a cave. Mammoth remains include bones, teeth, ivory tusks, pieces of fossilized skeletons, entire **mummified** or frozen bodies, and mammoth dung, not to mention carved bone and ivory objects and cave paintings of mammoths created by early humans.

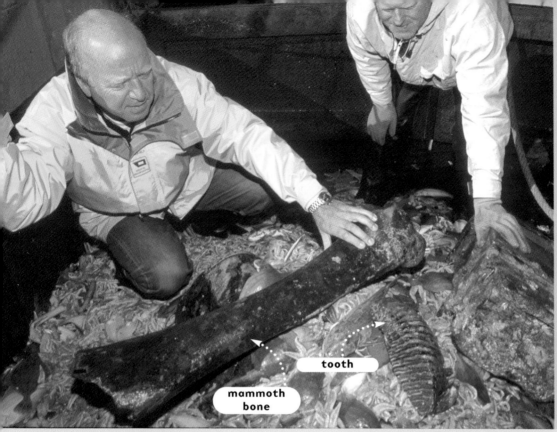

mammoth bone

tooth

While dragging nets along the bottom of the North Sea in Europe, Dutch fishing ships in the 1800s often caught mammoth bones along with fish. They usually kept the fish and threw out the bones.

A fishing crew found these mammoth remains underwater. But this mammoth didn't wander into the sea and drown. It lived on solid ground, but water levels have risen nearly 400 feet (120 meters) since the animal's death.

Some caves in southern Europe contain evidence of contact between early humans and mammoths. Carved and painted wall decorations show living mammoths. Small fragments of carved tusks and objects made from mammoth bones have also been found in caves and at archaeological digs in Europe and Siberia.

Preserved mammoth remains are usually either frozen or fossilized. Fossils are traces or parts of an animal left behind and preserved in the earth's rocky crust. Few mammoths became fossilized, and only under very special conditions, such as when a mammoth died and was quickly covered in a certain kind of fine soil or mud. Unless the remains were carried off by a landslide or by moving water, mammoth fossils are usually found right where the animal died. Frozen mammoth remains are more likely to move as the surrounding ground thaws. Frozen remains can also be scattered by a river, eaten or gnawed upon by passing animals, or rotted in the sun. So the location of a frozen **carcass,** or body, is not always a good indicator of where the animal lived and died.

A Mammoth Mystery

For hundreds of years, people have struggled to explain the mammoth remains they've found. Were they sacred beasts or scary monsters? Should they be used for profit or for scientific study?

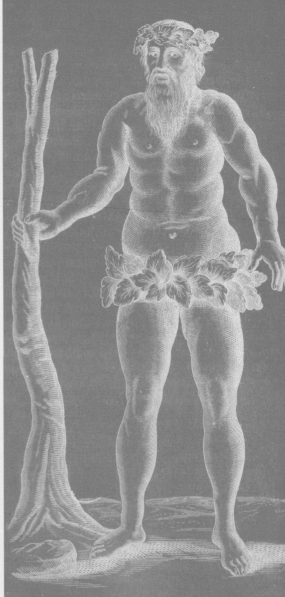

What Have We Got Here?

Imagine that you live in Siberia or Alaska years ago. During a spring thaw, a frozen mammoth slowly appears out of melting ice. No one has ever seen this animal alive, so people aren't sure what to think. Is it a beast that clawed its way up from underground, only to die in the light of the sun or moon? Or did this strange-looking creature rise up from the earth to help humans communicate with the dead?

In the past, many people who found mammoth remains were afraid to disturb them. What was found in the ground should stay there, they reasoned. They feared that moving the bones would disturb the spirits of the dead, and surely terrible things would happen then!

Mammoth tusks or bones have fascinated the people who have stumbled upon them. Some people have used the remains to make tools, while others have sold them. But most were too afraid to touch them.

Until the 1600s, most people who found mammoth bones had no idea what kind of animal might have left behind such huge remains. Had they found the skull of a Cyclops—a mythical one-eyed giant? Were these the bones of human giants? Were they fakes meant to look like real animal bones, or bits of unicorn skeleton? Some Christians considered the bones to be holy and took care to preserve and display them in castles, palaces, cathedrals, and monasteries.

Each new discovery of mammoth remains helps scientists learn more about this extinct animal. At the same time, stories, beliefs, and superstitions about mammoths continue to be passed down from generation to generation.

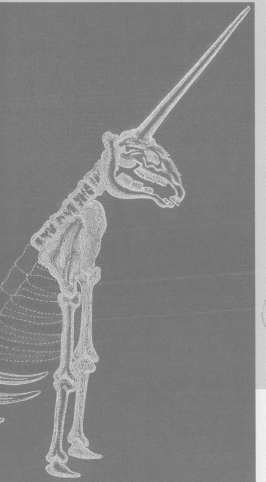

Reconstructing now-extinct animals based on incomplete skeletons and other evidence has always been a challenge. Some of the first people to study mammoth remains drew bizarre beasts with some familiar features: cattle with great curving horns, wild boars with ivory mustaches. None of these creatures had trunks, simply because trunks hadn't been found on any of the carcasses discovered up to that point.

In the 1700s, scholars began to study woolly mammoth remains in more detail. They could see the similarities between mammoths and elephants. But how did these bones end up in Europe and Siberia, when elephants live in the warmer climates of Africa and Asia? Could these beasts have descended from elephants that were taken from Africa in ancient times? No. Scientist Georges Cuvier proved that these animals were slightly different from elephants and had disappeared long ago. In 1799, the woolly mammoth received a scientific name: *Elephas primigenius,* which means "forerunner of the elephant." That scientific name was later changed to *Mammuthus primigenius.*

Tracking Down Mammoths in the 1900s

For scientists and scholars in the early 1900s, finding and studying woolly mammoth remains was no easy task.

More than anything, the search for mammoth remains required an adventurous spirit, since it usually involved traveling for months over thousands of miles of frozen ground.

The first sign of a new discovery often came when a reindeer hunter arrived in a Siberian village with ivory mammoth tusks for sale.

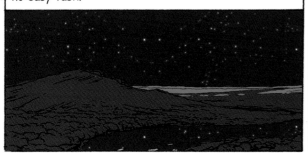

The information quickly found its way to the ears of scientists...

officials...

the local governor...

and even the czar.

It took time for the scientists to gather permits, money, supplies, and workers. Then the expedition set off to find and remove the frozen remains.

The scientists, along with a guide, an interpreter, an artist, and natives of the area, started out on a dangerous ten-month journey, traveling by...

train...

boat...

horseback...

wagon, sled, and on foot, all the way to the site of the original discovery. They carried everything they needed with them: food, guns, gloves, collapsible boats that also served as tents, and tools for breaking ice.

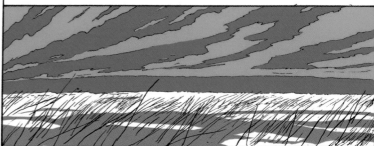

Once the excitement of finding the carcass passed, people quickly set to work organizing a base camp. This would be their home for weeks to come.

The first step in removing the frozen remains was to build a wooden frame around the carcass. The crew set fires around the carcass to speed the thawing process.

Workers spent weeks digging deeper and deeper to free the animal...

while trying to forget their superstitions and fighting off wild animals that were attracted by the smell of the thawing, and now decomposing, mammoth.

There was only one way to move such a large carcass: cut it into smaller pieces.

Once the animal was free of the ice, workers took the rotting meat and organs not yet eaten by scavengers, and wrapped them in cow or horse hides...

let them refreeze in the open air, then placed them in cases.

These cases were stacked on sleds pulled by dogs, reindeer, or horses. They were finally ready to head home.

During the difficult return journey, these poor animals pulled and pulled and pulled...

and slid over the ice and snow. Some sleds lost their loads. The crew repacked the load and kept going.

At last, the crew arrived at the museum in St. Petersburg, Russia. Here the mammoth carcass could be studied...

assembled, then proudly presented to the public.

Tracking Down Mammoths Today

Since the early 1900s, methods for bringing frozen woolly mammoth remains to the laboratory have changed dramatically.

Among the 4.5 tons (4 metric tons) of supplies and other materials brought to the site, you'll find everything needed to feed and warm the crew, including: food and drinks, heaters, mattresses, sleeping bags, and tents designed for extreme cold.

The people and materials for the trip can be pulled together in a matter of days and transported by plane, freighter, truck, bus, 4x4 vehicle, ultralight aircraft, helicopter, snowmobile, or sled.

What a Find!

When reindeer herders accidentally discover a mammoth carcass during their travels in Siberia, the location of the remains is pinpointed precisely on maps. Officials let scientists and specialists in the region know about the find.

Packing for the Trip

To locate, remove, and transport a carcass, all kinds of tools are needed: GPS (Global Positioning System) devices, radar, shovels, electric generators, air compressors, impact drills, steel pry bars and cables, cranes, extra fuel—and cameras to preserve the memories of the discovery. Radios allow contact with the outside world, and a helicopter arrives every week with mail and additional supplies.

Thanks to the telephone, fax machine, and computer, a few dozen technicians and scientists from several different countries can be brought together quickly:

paleontologists   **archaeologists**   **biologists**   **microbiologists**   **taxonomists**

In 1999, mammoth remains weighing as much as 22 tons (20 metric tons) were transported by air, like a huge ice cube, from the site where they were found. The carcass (named the Jarkov mammoth, after the person who discovered it) was placed in a permafrost tunnel in Russia where the temperature stays at 5° Fahrenheit (-15° Celsius). There, researchers from around the world can study the remains for years to come.

Handling the Carcass

In the past, workers frequently used pressurized water hoses to scour carcasses clean—and quickly get at the skeletons inside. Today, scientists work carefully to conserve all of the animal remains and even the surrounding soil. They work quickly and neatly, so remains don't thaw or become contaminated.

Each find—even a small piece of bone or skin—can provide precious clues about how mammoths lived.

geologists

experts in ancient geography

workers

photographers

cooks

A Visit to the Laboratory

Different remains collected in the field come together at laboratories, where researchers will study them. But first, they need to be cleaned, identified, and stored.

Bones brought to the laboratory are carefully cleaned.

Scientists draw them, measure them, and then try to determine the animal's species, age, and sex.

Scientists study frozen mammoth carcasses piece by piece, slowly thawing each piece in order to avoid damaging the remains.

The hide is tanned and stored in a dry, insect-free environment.

Objects made by prehistoric humans from pieces of mammoth bone or tusk arrive at the laboratory in plastic bags filled with cotton.

Drawings of mammoths found in caves are photographed and measured.

In the 1800s, people traced right over the drawings. Today, people try not to touch them directly.

Next, the surface of the bone is studied under a magnifying glass or microscope to identify each mark and scratch: hyena teeth-marks, burned areas, or marks made by the stone tools of prehistoric humans while cutting off meat or gathering bone marrow.

Minerals in the bones are sometimes measured in order to find out if the animal lacked certain essential foods. After study, bones are covered in a protective, strengthening varnish. Then they are numbered and stored so that they can be found easily later on.

Organs such as the stomach and intestines are **dissected.** Their structure and their contents are analyzed and compared to those of other animals. This is how scientists determine what mammoths ate.

Each thawed portion is preserved in a chemical solution called formaldehyde, then labeled and stored.

They are carefully cleaned using small, soft brushes. Scientists remove dust and examine each piece closely with a magnifying glass or microscope for traces of wear and for any engravings on the surface.

Objects may also be x-rayed. X-rays can help scientists identify the kinds of tools used to make the object—and even the ways in which the tools were held.

Objects are labeled and stored in a dry environment where the temperature does not change much.

Instead, an artist works with measurements and photographs to make an exact copy of each cave drawing. In the laboratory, scientists compare the drawings to those found in other caves. Specialists work to understand what the drawings might mean.

Spreading the News

New discoveries are reported in scientific magazines and major newspapers. The least fragile portions of new mammoth finds are even put on display for the public to see.

Shape and Size

Only by closely studying bones from skeletons and comparing them to those of modern animals can scientists begin to imagine the woolly mammoth's great shape and size.

A Jigsaw Puzzle

Piecing together the skeleton of a mammoth from a pile of bones is not easy. Mammoth bones differ greatly in size and are very heavy. One by one, scientists must examine the bones, describe them, try to identify them, and place them in the correct position—telling front from back, top from bottom. Scientists must then put the bones together like pieces of a puzzle. Next, they attach the bones to a metal frame and lift the entire skeleton to a standing position.

In 1808 in St. Petersburg, Russia, the first mammoth skeleton was assembled and put on public display. The tusks, which were bought separately from the body, almost certainly belonged to a different animal. The position of the tusks and the shape of the back were corrected in the 1800s and 1900s, as scientists learned more about mammoths from new discoveries.

Specific parts of the skeleton help scientists determine a mammoth's age and sex. For example, the tusks of male mammoths are usually more curved, larger, and heavier than those of females. But the pelvic bones of a female are bigger than those of a male. In younger animals, the ends of longer bones are not completely formed.

At the front of the skull, an enormous "keyhole"-shaped opening is the mammoth's version of a nose. Modern animals with trunks have the same kind of nose opening in their skulls. This is how scientists first confirmed that mammoths had trunks.

With such big, solid bodies and long tusks, adult mammoths in good health did not need to worry about predators, or enemies, attacking them.

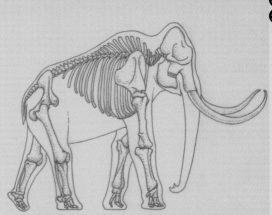

Like elephants, mammoths had more than just skin over their bones. Powerful muscles joined together the pieces of skeleton. Onto this layer of muscle, add a layer each of fat and skin to cover the skeleton, and you can begin to imagine the mammoth's true shape and size.

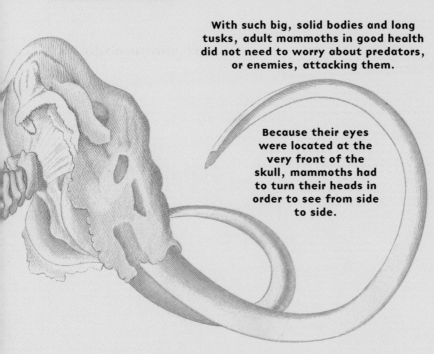

Because their eyes were located at the very front of the skull, mammoths had to turn their heads in order to see from side to side.

Try This On for Size!

The biggest woolly mammoths discovered thus far measured 10 to 13 feet tall (3 to 4 meters) at the shoulder. They weighed between 4.5 and 6.6 tons (4 to 6 metric tons). That's as much as 200 small children! The woolly mammoth has other impressive measurements, too: Its skull weighed more than 660 pounds (300 kilos). One tusk weighed as much as 100 to 175 pounds (45 to 80 kilos) and measured 8 to 13 feet (2.5 to 4 meters) long. Its trunk weighed 220 pounds (100 kilos) and was more than 6.5 feet (2 meters) long.

Mammoths on the Move

With such a heavy skeleton and with leg bones that stacked up like columns, the mammoth could not gallop like a horse or climb trees. It must have walked more like elephants, by moving the two right legs together, then the two left legs. Its toes touched the ground before its heels.

When putting together the first mammoth skeletons, experts could not decide how to position the tusks. There were several possible solutions—but some seemed more likely than others!

Tusks, Hair, and Hide

With its large, curving tusks, heavy fur coat, thick layer of fat, small ears, and short tail, the woolly mammoth wore the perfect outfit for survival in a cold climate.

a sloping back—strong but a bit stiff

tough skin, up to 1 inch (2.5 centimeters) thick

a layer of fat, from 3 to 4 inches (8 to 10 centimeters) thick, all over the body. This allowed the animal to store energy for winter and protected its internal organs from the outside cold.

a small tail, made longer by extra-thick hairs that measured about 2 feet (60 centimeters) long. The tail could move in all directions to chase away mosquitoes.

an anal valve at the base of the tail. This large fold of skin, 7 inches (18 centimeters) thick, covered the anus when not in use.

a top layer of downy fur, with hairs measuring 1 to 3 inches (2.5 to 8 centimeters) long. This dense coat trapped a thin layer of air next to the skin that protected the body from extreme temperatures.

underneath the downy fur, a mop of stiff hairs of all sizes, six times thicker than our hair

a layer of horn under the feet, which acted as a shock absorber and protected the feet from the frozen ground

A mammoth might have looked spiffy in barrettes and bows, but it was probably plain brown.

a hump on the shoulders and back that contained a little fat

a large, knob-like dome on the head that also had fat inside

slender ears that were covered with fur, particularly the areas that were exposed to wind. The mammoth's ears were one-fifth the size of the Asian elephant's.

strong, pointed tusks that were capable of breaking ice, clubbing other animals, and tossing carnivores in the air. The tusks grew throughout the mammoth's life, sometimes nearly 6 inches (15 centimeters) per year.

a heavy yet flexible trunk, which could hit and break the back of an attacking animal. The trunk also served as the animal's nose and lips.

Fur Facts

All parts of the woolly mammoth's body were covered in fur. Some of it probably fell out in spring and grew back at the beginning of the following winter.

Mammoth hairs discovered thus far have varied in color from yellowish blond to brown-gray-black, with some orange and red. After having been preserved for thousands of years, the natural colors of the hairs have been partially destroyed. We cannot know the exact color of woolly mammoths. But we can guess. Brown was very fashionable 10,000 years ago with musk oxen—and probably with mammoths, too.

MAMMOTH HAIR LENGTH

On flanks: 3 feet (90 cm)

On back: 16–18 inches (40–45 cm)

On knees: 14 inches (35 cm)

On shoulders and thighs: 15 inches (38 cm)

On feet: 6–7 inches (15–18 cm)

What's for Dinner?

Woolly mammoths were extremely large. To maintain their size, they searched for and ate food all day long. But what exactly did they eat?

In and Out

Mammoths were vegetarians, or **herbivores**. Every day, they gulped down about 20 gallons (80 liters) of water and 440 pounds (200 kilograms) of a variety of grasses. Sometimes they ate other plant matter, such as small flowering plants, tree buds, or bark.

Like African elephants today, they could deposit about 24 pounds (11 kilograms) of dung every two hours, which adds up to 200 to 300 pounds (90 to 135 kilograms) per day.

In mammoth dung, and in the intestines, stomachs, and mouths of frozen carcasses, scientists have found grasses, bits of stems, leaves, wood, flowers, pollen grains, fruit, and spores that were swallowed by mammoths.

front

crown

back

root

ADULT MAMMOTH MOLARS

length: 12 inches (30 cm)
width: 3 inches (8 cm)
height: 6 inches (15 cm)
weight: 6.6 pounds (3 kg)

The mammoth's four molars were located one on either side of its mouth, on both the top and bottom jaws. These molars stuck out from the gums only by about 1 inch (2.5 centimeters). On the surface, ridges of hard enamel surrounded the tender parts of the teeth. When mammoths moved their lower jaw from front to back, the molars scraped one against the other and ground up tough plant matter before the animal swallowed.

Grabbing a Bite to Eat

The mammoth's small neck kept it from grazing directly from the ground as cows do. To reach its food, it used its trunk and tusks. Based on the scratched and broken tusks that have been found, scientists believe that mammoths scraped the ground with their tusks to dig up plants or to tear off tree bark.

Using the tip of its trunk, a mammoth could delicately gather the smallest of flowers.

Chew on This

The mammoth had four enormous teeth called **molars.** These teeth grew continuously until the ridges were scraped smooth. Fortunately, by the time one set of molars was worn out, another was already in place. During a mammoth's lifetime, its molars replaced themselves five times. The first set was present at birth. Other sets followed at about 6 months, 4 years, 10 years, 20 years, and 35 years of age. Each new set of molars was larger than the one before and had more ridges.

At about sixty years of age, the mammoth's last set of molars fell out, and the animal eventually died of hunger.

A Handy Tool

The trunk was made up of thousands of small muscles. Thanks to this multi-purpose tool, the mammoth could breathe, touch, sniff, and drink. The trunk could also be pulled in or stretched out in all directions. Mammoths used their trunk to wrap around tufts of grasses, pull them up, and stuff them into their mouth. They also used their trunk to pull, push, lift, or tear off branches.

Home Sweet Habitat

Analyzing the foods the woolly mammoth ate has allowed scientists to begin reconstructing its **habitat,** the place where an animal normally lives.

Geography Lesson

Studying the land where a carcass or bone was found helps to complete the picture of the mammoth's habitat. Gravel would indicate that swiftly flowing rivers or glaciers were nearby. Sand and silt suggest slowly moving rivers. Clay would mark the location of a lake.

Przewalski's horse

saiga antelope

Some animals from the time of the mammoth are still living today, particularly in northern climates. They include the caribou, elk or red deer, moose, roe deer, ibex, chamois, wild boar, horse, brown bear, gray wolf, wild dog (dhole), red fox, arctic fox, leopard, and Eurasian lynx.

Most woolly mammoths lived during the **Pleistocene epoch,** a period of time which began 1.8 million years ago and ended about 10,000 years ago. This epoch had several long periods of very cold weather. The last of these cold periods, or Ice Ages, happened 21,000 years ago. At that time, woolly mammoths lived in a very dry and very cold climate. Temperatures were colder by an average of ten degrees.

Cool Scenery

Mammoths lived in a vast, flat landscape called a **steppe.** The steppe was covered in a variety of short grasses. A few trees dotted the banks of rivers and streams. The weather was cold, windy, and dry, with little rain or snow. Below the surface, the ground stayed frozen year round. In summer, only the surface thawed, and mammoths waded through mud puddles.

Other animals have completely disappeared:

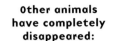

cave bear

cave hyena

steppe bison

giant deer

woolly rhinoceros

cave lion

wild ox

grouse

musk oxen

wolverine

collared lemming

Spring Birthdays

Asian elephants reproduce throughout the year. But among African elephants, babies are usually born during the rainy season, when there is plenty of food. Baby mammoths most likely were born during the relatively lush, green days of spring, nearly two years after their parents mated.

During the mating season, adult males joined up with a group of females. The males picked fights with each other to prove their strength and to attract the females.

Baby Care

A young mammoth drank milk from its mother's breasts, which were located between her front legs. At first, the baby drank with its mouth. By about five months of age, the young mammoth learned to use its trunk for drinking—and for picking plants.

A mother mammoth nursed her young for two to three years. After that time, she could have another baby. If a mother died before her baby was weaned, other mothers in the group would adopt the orphan.

We Are Family

No concrete evidence has survived to tell us about the family life of woolly mammoths. But we can imagine what their behavior might have been like by looking at elephant families today.

One frozen carcass has told us a lot about the youngest mammoths. This baby, called Dima, measured 27 inches (70 cm) tall and weighed 154 pounds (70 kg). Dima's back was rounded—the humps on the head and shoulders had not yet formed. It had tusks measuring just 2 inches (5 cm) long. Like a human's baby teeth, these "milk tusks" would have fallen out when the adult tusks came in.

Sticking Together

The family group was made up of about fifteen females and their babies. All the members were related: sisters, cousins, aunts, nieces, mothers, and daughters. The oldest mammoth was the leader. Young males stayed with the females for a dozen years. Then, gradually, they left the group to roam the steppe, alone or with other young males. The following summer, when it was time to mate, they joined a group of unrelated females.

When Mammoths Met People

Humans and mammoths lived during the same time period. Discoveries in the 1800s proved this. Neanderthals or Cro-Magnons (early humans) left behind carvings of woolly mammoths on bones and drew paintings on the rock walls of caves in Europe.

Most often, prehistoric humans simply stumbled upon the frozen carcasses of dead mammoths during their travels. They stored extra bones near their camps. These bones may have come from mammoths that had died thousands of years earlier.

Daring prehistoric hunters singled out a weak or solitary mammoth and directed it toward a trap. There they hit it with spears or stones. Hunters may have then cut either the ankles or the trunk and waited until the animal died of blood loss.

The many colors in these cave drawings come from natural pigments such as charcoal, manganese dioxide, ochre, iron oxide, and clay. Artists made the pigments into powders, then mixed them with water or heated them to make paint.

Painting the Mammoth

Prehistoric humans carved and painted pictures of mammoths on the rock walls and ceilings of caves. The styles and materials used in these pictures varied from region to region. To decorate the ceilings, artists climbed up scaffolding made from wood. They lit the dark caves with torches or small oil lamps. Nose to the wall, they wouldn't have been able to see the whole picture, as they would from farther away. They spread colors with their fingers, their hands, bunches of moss, tufts of hair or grasses, chewed sticks, or hollowed-out bones.

Hidden Meanings

Researchers are trying to figure out why artists chose where and what to draw. Were the artists hunters who believed that magic rituals and drawings would protect them? Were they trying to contact animals in the spirit world? Researchers are still debating these questions. What is certain is that prehistoric humans could think and express themselves through drawings.

GROCERY DEPARTMENT

1. Meat: back muscles, flanks and thighs, heart, tongue, trunk, feet... about 2.2 tons (2 metric tons) of meat per animal
2. Fat
3. Bone marrow
4. Cheap cooking fuel: bits of bone

ACCESSORIES

5. String and fine cord (tendons or hairs)
6. Purses (skin)
7. Blankets (skin)
8. Pocket-sized water bottle (cleaned intestines)
9. Flyswatters (furry tail)

TOOLS

10. Anvil (shoulder blade, for hammering on)
11. Sander (a whole molar)
12. Scraper for cleaning skins (a rib or carved ivory)
13. Shovel (carved thighbone)
14. Fish hook (carved ivory)
15. Digging stick (a rib or carved ivory)
16. Spatula (carved ivory)
17. Storage container (hollowed-out tusk)
18. Spoon or paddle (bone or carved ivory)
19. Needle (carved ivory)
20. Comb (carved ivory)
21. Pickaxe (sharpened tusk)
22. Scouring pad (carved molar)
23. Grinder (carved ivory)

HUNTING GEAR

A large selection of items in carved ivory or bone, much more durable than those made from reindeer bone
24. Hook for spear thrower (carved ivory)
25. Spear shaft (thighbone)
26. Knife (carved ivory)
27. Spear (carved ivory)
28. Javelin point (carved ivory)
29. Harpoon (carved ivory)
30. Boomerang (carved ivory)

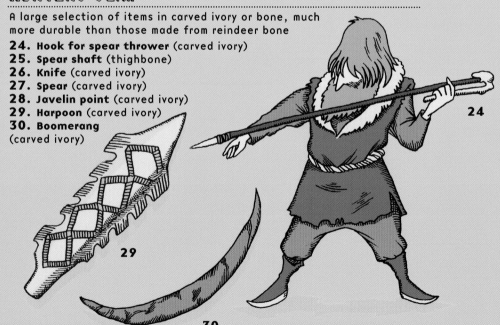

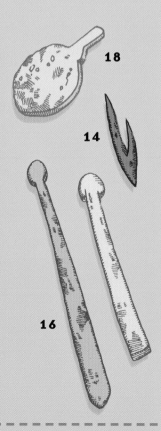

HOME IMPROVEMENT

31. Make-your-own-hut-kit. Build your own hut, with 215 square feet (20 m²) of livable space. Kit contains 385 bones (37 skulls, 35 pelvic bones, 30 thighbones and upper arm bones, 30 shoulder blades, 35 tusks, 95 jawbones, and an assortment of vertebrae), wooden posts, and skins. Total weight: 23 tons (21 t). Guaranteed for 15 years. Site requirements: should be nearly 16 feet (4.8 m) deep. Note: May take ten strong people five days to build.
32. Door (skin)

FURNITURE DEPARTMENT

33. Rug (skin)
34. Table (shoulder blade)
35. Chair (lower jawbone)
36. Lamp (fueled by mammoth fat)

33

23
34

JEWELRY AND HOME DÉCOR DEPARTMENT

37. A wide assortment of ivory or bone jewelry, including bracelets, barrettes, pins, buttons, beads, rings, necklaces, and earrings
38. One-of-a-kind sculptures and knickknacks (carved ivory, clay, or bone)
39. Wall and ceiling murals featuring mammoths in various scenes (by special order only)

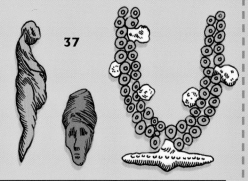
37

Mammoth Department Store

In the vast steppe regions, meetings between woolly mammoths and humans were fairly rare. But when humans managed to bring down one of these beasts, they made use of even the smallest bits of the carcass. As you can see, the wide range of products they made could have stocked a department store!

FUNERAL SUPPLIES

40. Fine grave covers (shoulder blade, fragment of pelvic bone)

MUSIC DEPARTMENT

41. Percussion instruments (tusk, shoulder blade, skull, pelvis)
42. Flute (hollowed-out thighbone)
43. Triangle (ivory rings)

Dear Mammoth Diary

Scientists know from studying the condition of bones and teeth that life for woolly mammoths wasn't all fun and games. Every day, they risked illness and deadly accidents. Too bad no mammoths left behind a record of their days.

Here is what one young woolly mammoth *might* have written in his diary:

May 16

I had a close call last week. I fell in the river when I was trying to pull a branch from a birch tree. My mother had to grab me and pull me out of the icy water. I guess I was lucky.

Then, today, one of my big brothers fell into a hole. He tried to get back out, but it was too deep. He broke some bones and was hurting pretty bad. Before we could rescue him, a mud slide covered him. We figure he died because he couldn't get enough air to breathe. He never even had time to swallow the grass he had in his mouth.

April 27

This morning, I slipped in a mud puddle. Some strange animals ran after me, making noise and holding pointed sticks. But I hid behind my big cousin.

October 3
I don't like fall. There are fewer flowers, and it starts getting cold. And I'm itchy all over. Mosquitoes and lice won't leave me alone. Pretty soon my old aunties start complaining the way they always do. There's always something wrong with them: an elbow that sticks, a knee that swells up, a toothache, tusks that are twisted or broken, even problems going to the bathroom...Me, since I didn't eat much last year, my tusks haven't grown as much as they should have. I might even get cavities in my teeth later. But that's better than having teeth that are all worn down, like Grandma's!

June 18
Now I'm big, and I want to leave this group of females and travel. The steppe is so huge. I'm sure to find a nice girlfriend somewhere out there. I'll have to be careful not to get lost. And I'll need to cross some rivers. But that doesn't scare me anymore, now that I know how to swim a little.

The End of Mammoths

All species of mammoths have disappeared, like many other large mammals of the same era. Researchers are trying to figure out why they became extinct.

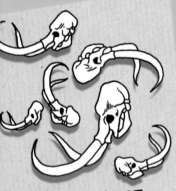

WHEN THE LAST MAMMOTHS DIED: THE FIGURES

Bones collected throughout the Northern Hemisphere indicate that woolly mammoths (who lived to be 60 to 80 years old) died in great numbers 10,000 to 12,000 years ago. Other mammoth species were also extinct by about this time.

Some mammoth bones are more recent, dating from 3,700 to 7,000 years ago. These small bones were found on Wrangel Island, in the Arctic Ocean, and belong to dwarf woolly mammoths.

Of Mice and Mammoths: What's the Difference?

On the same amount of land, you might find one thousand times more mice (prehistoric mice, that is) than woolly mammoths. In five years', two mice that were just a few months old could give birth to several hundred little mice. But two mammoths (each more than 15 years old) could produce only one or two babies during that time. If a few individuals died, the mice population would not be affected at all, but the mammoth population might have trouble surviving.

Have We Finally Found the Culprits?

Could humans have caused mammoths to become extinct? Scientists continue to discuss the possibility. The rapid growth of the human population and the development of better hunting tools might, in part, explain the disappearance of mammoths. The invention of spear points made from sharpened stone allowed hunters to pierce tough skins and to kill large animals. But no group of hunters, no matter how skilled, could have killed so many animals over such a large area in less than two thousand years.

OTHER, LESS LIKELY THEORIES
People have come up with many disaster theories—including comets, asteroids, bacteria, viruses, and terrible diseases—to explain the extinction of woolly mammoths. But none of these theories has been confirmed.

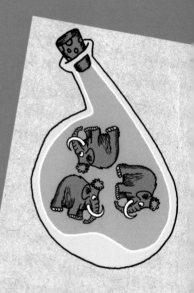

Bringing Mammoths Back: Fact or Fiction?
For the moment, we cannot clone, or scientifically re-create, woolly mammoths. The DNA found in frozen carcasses has broken down or is incomplete. Nonetheless, American, Japanese, and European researchers are still trying to create a modern mammoth. But should we spend so much energy and money trying to bring back an extinct animal, who, if we succeed in reviving him, would have no place to live? It's worth remembering that while these experiments move forward, thousands of elephants face the threat of extinction.

Did the Thermometer Do It?
Fifteen thousand years ago, at the end of the last Ice Age, the climate grew warmer and glaciers began to melt. In one thousand years, temperatures increased six degrees. Rains came more frequently, and the level of water in the oceans rose, reducing the size of continents. Forests in the south of Europe spread into the north and east, breaking up or replacing the steppe, the woolly mammoth's traditional habitat. Mammoths might have disappeared because they had a harder time finding food. Many predators—also starving—disappeared as well.

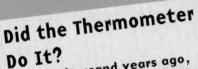

The Best Explanation Yet
Scientists who support the different theories continue to disagree. But today most believe that changes in vegetation, or plant life, forced the last woolly mammoths into smaller and smaller areas on the steppe. There, prehistoric humans finished them off. But new discoveries may change that explanation.

Close Relatives

Woolly mammoths were not alone. Close examination of fossils proves that several species of mammoth existed around the world over millions of years. They or their ancestors began migrating from Africa into Europe, Asia, and North America almost three million years ago.

While roaming the world, mammoths gradually evolved. Slowly their size increased, and their trunks and tusks grew longer. At the same time, their faces became flatter and their skulls became rounder.

EUROPE

AFRICA

The oldest and smallest mammoth species—*Mammuthus africanavus* and *Mammuthus subplanifrons* lived in North and East Africa.

African ancestor

These are the major mammoth species:

The Columbian mammoth, *Mammuthus columbi*, lived in North America during the same time period as the woolly mammoth, but it had no woolly coat. It was bigger and heavier, and it stuffed itself with leaves torn from trees in scattered forests. Some individuals from the two species may have met in Alaska.

The steppe mammoth, *Mammuthus trogontherii*, lived in grassy and tree-covered regions of Europe and Siberia. This was the biggest mammoth of them all. It was 13 feet (4 meters) tall and weighed at least 11 tons (10 metric tons).

The southern mammoth, *Mammuthus meridionalis*, lived mainly in the temperate forests of Eurasia but also traveled as far as North America.

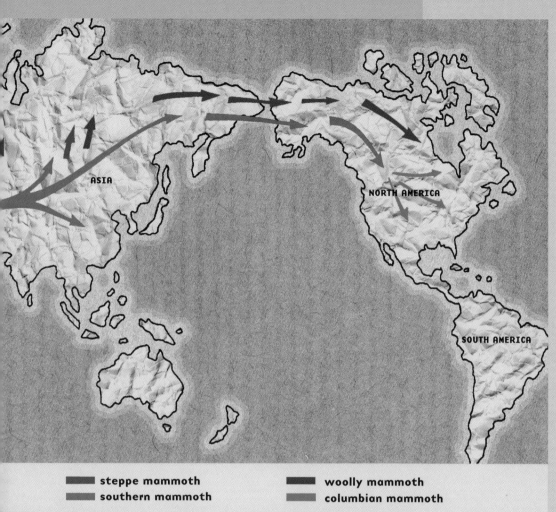

ASIA

NORTH AMERICA

SOUTH AMERICA

About 2.7 million years ago, mammoths in East Africa slowly moved north. Their successors lived in Europe, Asia, Siberia, and even North America. In Eurasia, these early mammoths evolved into steppe mammoths. In North America, the Columbian mammoths evolved. Woolly mammoths came after steppe mammoths, and some traveled as far as Alaska, crossing a land bridge that once existed at the modern-day Bering Strait. No mammoths have been found in South America, but Columbian mammoths, including dwarfs of that species, have been found on the Channel Islands off the coast of California.

| steppe mammoth | woolly mammoth |
| southern mammoth | columbian mammoth |

Elephant Relatives . . .

The woolly mammoth belongs to the order of animals known as proboscideans (animals with trunks). Today there are only two species of proboscideans: the African elephant and the Asian elephant. The mammoth is not their ancestor. They are more like cousins.

manatee

hyrax

And others?

Apart from elephants, the animals that come closest to mammoths don't look much like them, but they have several characteristics in common. Manatees and dugongs (sea cows) have identical hearts. Their breasts are also in the same location as those of mammoths. Hyrax, which resemble guinea pigs, have ears and rear feet like those of mammoths.

Where Did Mammoths Live?

The last mammoth species—woolly mammoths and Columbian mammoths—lived in Eurasia and North America. Nearly all

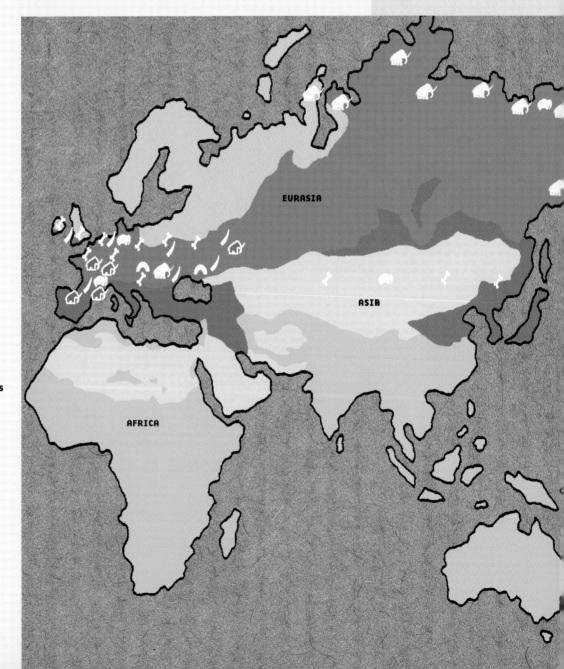

woolly mammoth bone

frozen woolly mammoth remains

Columbian mammoth remains

drawings of mammoths

statues of mammoths

objects made from mammoth bone and tusk

traces of huts made from mammoth bones

continental glaciers

steppe

forests and **savannas**

southern steppe and deserts

subtropics and tropics

EURASIA

ASIA

AFRICA

mammoths died out by about 10,000 years ago, but some dwarf mammoths survived 6,000 years longer on isolated islands. This map shows where evidence of these mammoths has been found.

WRANGEL ISLAND

NORTH AMERICA

SOUTH AMERICA

Have Mammoths Really Disappeared?

In 1920, a hunter in the forests of Siberia reported seeing an enormous elephant with curved tusks. He also saw footprints and a large pile of dung. In 1944, pilots flying over Alaska located large beasts living alone or in herds. In 1956, a schoolteacher caught sight of an enormous animal. In 1962, another hunter saw one. These statements are disturbing, and even if there were video evidence, they would be difficult to believe. In any case, there are thousands of real fossilized and frozen mammoths, still hidden in the ground and snow.

Since the disappearance of the mammoth, the climate has changed a great deal. The Ice Ages of the Pleistocene epoch have ended, and habitats are completely different. The great grassy steppe of Eurasia, home to many different animal species, no longer exists. In its place, there are now marshy tundra and taiga, forests of pine trees. These areas are home to modern reindeer, musk oxen, and horses, which look much like those that once lived alongside the woolly mammoth.

Tricky Trunk Spotting:
How to Tell a Mammoth from an Elephant

Here are the main similarities and differences among adult males of three different species: the woolly mammoth, the African elephant, and the Asian elephant.

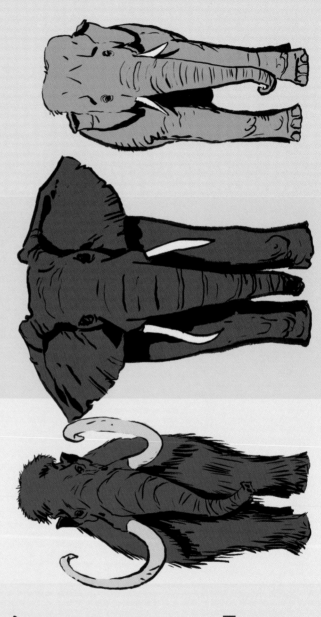

Woolly Mammoth

African Elephant

Asian Elephant

Which is the woolly mammoth's closest cousin? On the outside, the mammoth looks more like the Asian elephant than the African elephant. But on the inside, the opposite is the case. Scientists continue to study the animals at a molecular level (that is, under powerful microscopes) to settle the question once and for all.

	Mammuthus primigenius	Loxodonta africana	Elephas maximus
scientific name	Mammuthus primigenius	Loxodonta africana	Elephas maximus
height	9 to 11 feet (2.7 to 3.4 meters)	10 to 11 feet (3 to 3.4 meters)	8 to 10 feet (2.4 to 3 meters)
weight	4.5 to 6.6 tons (4 to 6 metric tons)	4.4 to 6.6 tons (4 to 6 metric tons)	3.3 to 5.5 tons (3 to 5 metric tons)
head shape	raised, dome-like	low, dome-like	2 forward humps
type of ears	very small	large	medium
end of trunk	1 flat tip, 1 long tip	2 long tips	1 long tip
type of tusks	curved, spiral	gently curved	gently curved
back shape	slopes down from shoulder to tail	dips in the middle	humped
hair	thick	very sparse	sparse
size of tail	short	long	long
diet	grasses, herbaceous plants, twigs, bark	leaves, twigs, branches, fruit	grasses, water-rich plants, bamboo, rice, sugarcane
habitat	open spaces: frozen, grassy steppe	open spaces: grassy savanna with scattered forest	sheltered spaces: dense tropical forest
distribution	Northern Hemisphere: Eurasia, North America	central Africa	Southeast Asia (India, Ceylon, Malaysia, Burma, Thailand, Indochina, Borneo, Sumatra)
status	lived 600,000 to 4,000 years ago. Now extinct	endangered	endangered

Test Your Mammoth Knowledge

Q: What is the Latin name of the woolly mammoth?

-Mammuthus minigenius
-Mammuthus primigenius
-Mammuthus primi-jello-ous

A: Mamumuthus primigenius. See page 11.

Q: What can you not make out of pieces of mammoth?

-rugs, tables, houses
-bracelets, axes, spoons
-tires, windows, coffeemakers

A: Tires, windows, and coffeemakers. See pages 30 to 31.

Q: What do reindeer hunters do when they discover woolly mammoth tusks?

-make a good profit selling the tusks
-say a prayer and skedaddle
-carve a nice comb out of the tusks to give to a girlfriend

A: All three answers are possible. It all depends on the hunter. See pages 8 to 10.

Q: The trunk of an adult woolly mammoth is...

-More than 3 feet (1 meter) long and weighs 55 pounds (25 kilograms)
-5 feet (1.5 meters) long and weighs 110 pounds (50 kilograms)
-More than 6.5 feet (2 meters) long and weighs 220 pounds (100 kilograms)

A: The trunk is more than 6.5 feet (2 meters) long and weighs 220 pounds (100 kilograms). See page 19.

Q: True or False? Mammoths hid behind trees in the forest.

A: False. They were way too big for that. See pages 24 to 25.

Q: Scientists have dissected mammoth dung because:

-they think it's funny
-they hope to find clues about the mammoth's diet
-it's a nice change after dissecting lab mice

A: They hope to find clues about the mammoth's diet. See pages 22 to 23.

Q: True or False? Mammoths got cavities.

A: True. See page 33.

Q: True or False? The woolly mammoth has hairs on its feet that are 6 inches (15 centimeters) long.

A: True. See page 21.

Q: True or False? Pregnant mammoths carried their young for almost two years.

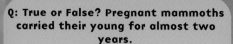

A: True...just as it is for elephants today. See page 26.

Q: What did mammoths do all day long?

-knit mammoth-hair sweaters
-played "hop over the bison"
-searched for plants to eat, and then ate them

A: They searched for plants to eat, and then ate them. See page 22.

Q: True or False? With a helicopter, you can lift a block of ice weighing 22 tons (20 metric tons) and containing an entire frozen woolly mammoth.

A: True. See page 15.

Q: The hair of the woolly mammoth must have been...

-white like Santa Claus's beard
-brown like that of musk oxen
-golden like wheat

A: It was most likely brown, like that of musk oxen. See page 21.

Q: True or False? Prehistoric humans scribbled on the walls and ceilings of their caves.

A: True...and false, because they didn't just scribble. They were true artists! See page 29.

Q: True or False? Mammoths dug underground caverns.

A: False. But humans dig in the ground sometimes to gather fossilized mammoth remains. See page 10.

Q: To preserve a mammoth skin, scientists put it:

-in water
-in oil
-in a dry place, away from insects

A: Skins are stored in a dry place, away from insects. See page 16.

Q: True or False? Woolly mammoths were afraid of lemmings.

A: Scientists have no evidence either way, but you never know...!

Q: Where did the very last of the mammoths live?

-in warm tropical forests
-on an uninhabited island
-in a cage at the zoo

A: Dwarf woolly mammoths lived on Wrangel Island until 4,000 years ago. See page 34.

Q: True or False? Mammoths are still alive today.

A: False, at least until someone comes forward with proof to the contrary. See page 39.

Glossary

archaeologists: scientists who study the physical remains (such as fossils, monuments, and artifacts) of past human life

biologists: scientists who study plant and animal life

carcass: the body of a dead animal

DNA: an abbreviation of deoxyribonucleic acid, the molecule that carries an organism's genetic material

dissect: to carefully take apart something (such as a dead animal) to study it

dwarf mammoth: a subset of a mammoth species that, over time, had smaller and smaller members, usually as a response to limited food in a small habitat, such as an island. Dwarf woolly mammoths lived on Wrangel Island in the Arctic Ocean, while dwarf Columbian mammoths lived on the Channel Islands off the coast of California.

Eurasia: the name given to Europe and Asia as one continent

extinct: no longer living. A species becomes extinct when its last members die.

fossil: the trace or remnant of an animal left behind and preserved in the earth's crust

geologists: scientists who study the earth's history

habitat: the place where an animal normally lives and grows

herbivores: animals that eat only plants

Ice Age: a time, during the Pleistocene epoch, marked by the wide spread of glaciers, or large bodies of ice

microbiologists: scientists who study the smallest forms of plant and animal life

molars: teeth in the upper and lower jaws of some animals that enable them to grind their food

mummified: preserved by drying, as can happen with woolly mammoth remains in the very cold and dry conditions of Siberia

Northern Hemisphere: the half of the earth that lies north of the equator

paleontologists: scientists who study fossil remains to learn about past geological periods

Pleistocene epoch: a period of time, marked by cold periods called Ice Ages, which began 1.8 million years ago and ended about 10,000 years ago

proboscideans: large mammals that have long, flexible noses called trunks

savannas: tropical or subtropical grasslands with scattered trees

sinkhole: a depression in the ground caused by the collapse of an underground cave or by water wearing away the soil

species: a group of animals or organisms that have common traits and that can mate to produce healthy young

steppe: a vast, dry grassland with few or no trees

taiga: a cool, wet area of pine-tree forests

taxonomists: scientists who classify plants and animals

Index

More Mammoth Books, Videos, and Links

Books:

Agenbroad, Larry D., and Lisa Nelson. *Mammoths: Ice-Age Giants.* Lerner Publications Co., 2002.

Aliki. *Wild and Woolly Mammoths.* HarperCollins, 1997.

Arnold, Carolyn. *When Mammoths Walked the Earth.* Illustrated by Laurie Caple. Clarion, 2002.

Giblin, James Cross. *Mystery of the Mammoth Bones.* HarperCollins, 1999.

Miller, Debbie S. *A Woolly Mammoth Journey.* Illustrated by Jon Van Zyle. Little, Brown, 2001.

Videos:

The Hot Springs Mammoth Site. West River Video Productions, 1995.
Raising the Mammoth. Artisan Entertainment/Discovery Channel, 2001.
Walking with Prehistoric Beasts. BBC Video, 2002.

Links:

The Mammoth Site
www.mammothsite.com
Tells the story of the Hot Springs, SD, sinkhole in which many mammoths were trapped thousands of years ago.

Woolly Mammoth-Discovery School
http://school.discovery.com/schooladventures/woollymammoth/
Activities and information linked to a Discovery Channel documentary about the unearthing of the Jarkov mammoth remains in Siberia.